Solar Power

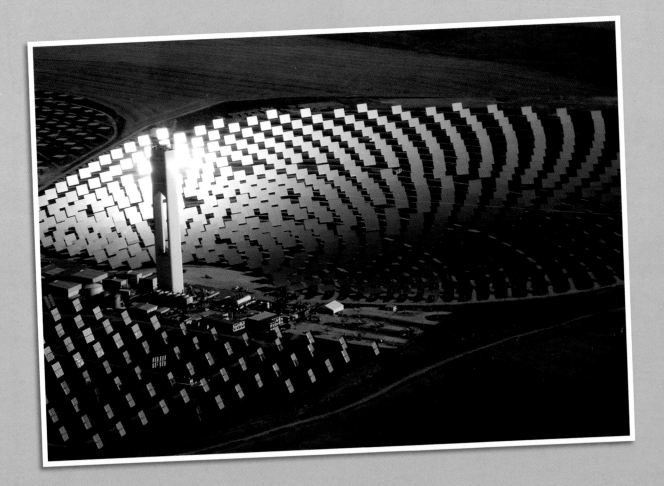

Richard and Louise Spilsbury

PowerKiDS
press.

New York

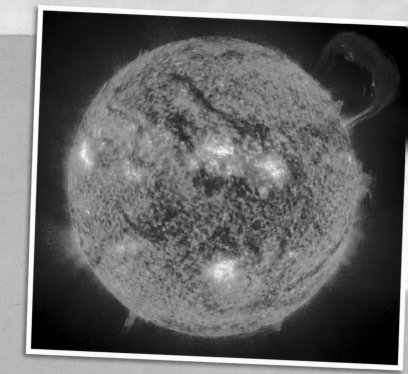

Published in 2012 by
The Rosen Publishing Group Inc.
29 East 21st Street,
New York, NY 10010

First Edition

Editorial Director: Rasha Elsaeed
Produced for Wayland by Discovery Books Ltd
Managing Editor: Rachel Tisdale
Designer: Ian Winton
Illustrator: Stefan Chabluk
Picture Researcher: Tom Humphrey

Library of Congress Cataloging-in-Publication Data

Spilsbury, Richard, 1963-
Solar power / by Richard Spilsbury and Louise Spilsbury. – 1st ed.
     p. cm. – (Let's discuss energy resources)
Includes index.
ISBN 978-1-4488-5262-8 (lib. bdg.)
1. Solar energy–Juvenile literature. I. Spilsbury, Louise. II. Title.
TJ810.3.S65 2012
333.792'3–dc22

2010046936

Photographs:
AORA: p. 9 (Haim Fried); Barefoot Photographers of Tilonia: p. 15 (Flickr); BP: p. 29 (Makai Construction);
Construction Photography: p. 5; Coolearth Solar: p. 27; Corbis: p. 24 (Jim Young/Reuters); Desert
Tec—UK (www.trec-uk.org.uk): p. 16 & title page (Sandia National Laboratories), p. 21 (Sandia National
Laboratories); Flickr: p. 26 (Gnal); Getty Images: p. 18 (Kay Chernush/The Image Bank); Helios Resource:
p. 22; NASA: p. 7 (ESA/SOHO), p. 14, p. 28 (Solar Impulse Company); NREL: p. 13 (Southern California
Edison); Photolibrary: p. 10 (Maximilian Stock Ltd.); Shutterstock: cover (Pinosub), p. 6 (Otmar Smit),
p. 11 (John Keith), p. 19 (Darren J Bradley), p. 20 (SphinxHK); SXC: p. 4 (www.sxc.hu).

Manufactured in China
CPSIA Compliance Information: Batch #WAS1102PK: For Further Information
contact Rosen Publishing, New York, New York at 1-800-237-9932

Contents

The words in **bold** can be found in the glossary on page 31.

Solar Power as an Energy Resource

We use energy resources every day, without thinking about it! Cars burn fuel in engines to release the energy that turns their wheels. Sun shining through greenhouse windows warms the air to help plants grow. From cell phones to DVD players, most of the machines we use run on electricity made using energy resources.

Energy Resources

Most of the energy that we use to make electricity comes from **fossil fuels**, such as coal, oil, and gas. These energy resources took millions of years to form underground from the buried remains of ancient plants and animals. Worldwide, about 67 percent of electricity is made in fossil fuel **power plants**, mostly from coal. These power plants burn fossil fuels to make heat energy that can be used to make electricity.

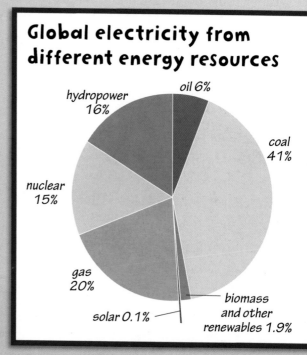

Global electricity from different energy resources

hydropower 16%

oil 6%

coal 41%

nuclear 15%

gas 20%

solar 0.1%

biomass and other renewables 1.9%

Problems with Fossil Fuels

One problem with fossil fuels is that there is a limited amount in the Earth. Scientists think that coal, oil, and gas could all run out within 200 years if we continue using as much electricity, and fuel in our vehicles, as we do today. Another problem is that burning fossil fuels to release heat also releases gases into the **atmosphere**.

The major problem with using fossil fuels to generate electricity is the production of **greenhouse gases** that build up in the atmosphere.

Some of these gases cause **pollution**, which can harm people and the environment. Others, such as **carbon dioxide** gas, are types of greenhouse gases that build up and store heat from the Sun in the atmosphere. Most scientists believe this is causing **global warming**, which is rapidly changing weather patterns across the world. This climate change is causing flooding and droughts.

Renewable Energy Resources

Renewable energy resources will not run out because they are in endless supply. These resources include sunlight, wind, waves, tides, and biomass. Biomass is renewable fuel made from plant and animal material, including wood, crops, and manure and some household garbage. Fossil fuels are **nonrenewable**, because they are not forming naturally as people use them up. Using renewable energy for power produces far less greenhouse gases and pollution than fossil fuels, so they are less harmful to our planet.

In this solar power station in Hemau, Bayern, Germany, hundreds of panels capture solar energy and turn it into electricity.

Why discuss solar power?

People have used the Sun's energy, or solar power, for thousands of years for warmth and light, but today we can also use it to make electricity. Globally, less than 1 percent of all electricity comes from solar power. This book explores the advantages and disadvantages of using solar power to meet our growing demand for electricity now and into the future.

How We Use the Sun's Energy

The Sun is millions of miles away from Earth, but it is still our nearest star. Like other stars, the Sun is an enormous ball of incredibly hot gases. Solar energy from the Sun's gases moves through space to Earth in the form of heat and light **radiation**. We can use the energy in the Sun's radiation in different ways.

Solar Heating

The simplest way in which we use the Sun's heat is to warm our homes. By building houses with windows that face the Sun, the glass lets heat radiation in to warm the air that is trapped inside. We can heat water using solar collectors. Solar collectors are large glass panels that go on house roofs. Inside the panels are dark pipes that contain liquid. The pipes absorb heat radiation from the Sun and warm the liquid inside. They carry the hot liquid inside the house to heat tanks of water.

Solar collectors absorb heat in sunlight and transfer this energy via liquids to water.

Electricity from the Sun

We can also make electricity using the Sun's energy in two ways. In a thermal solar power plant, sunlight is used to boil water, making high-pressure steam. The moving steam spins the blades of a **turbine**, which looks a little bit like a propeller. A machine called a generator then converts the movement energy, or **kinetic energy**, of the turbine into electrical energy. The second way to make electricity from sunlight is with **solar cells**. These are devices that change sunlight directly into electricity in one step.

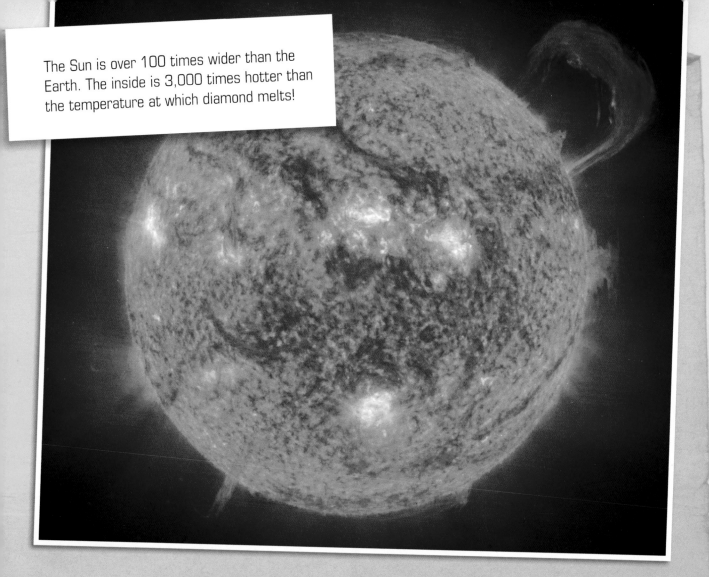

The Sun is over 100 times wider than the Earth. The inside is 3,000 times hotter than the temperature at which diamond melts!

Energy and Power

Energy is usually described as the ability to do work. A computer gets the energy it needs to work from electricity. Energy can be measured in units called joules. People often use the word "power" to mean a supply of electricity. Power is the rate at which energy is used or sent. It is measured in units called watts, which are joules per second. A laptop computer needs 45 watts to make it work. A kilowatt (kW) is 1,000 watts and a megawatt (MW) is 1 million watts.

We can compare how much electricity a home, business, or town uses or consumes using units that show the energy used each hour: the kilowatt hour (kWh) or megawatt hour (MW). People in different countries consume different amounts, depending on how many electrical machines they use. For example, in 2005, an average person in Canada used 17 MW, whereas an average person in Costa Rica used a tenth of this amount.

Thermal Solar Power Plants

Even on the hottest summer's day, sunlight on a puddle of water only makes it warm. Thermal solar power plants need a way of concentrating solar heat so it can superheat liquids. They use systems of mirrors to reflect, or bounce, sunlight that falls over a large area onto a small area. Then it can be used to make electricity.

Troughs

Some thermal solar plants use mirrors that are shaped like troughs. This shape reflects sunlight that hits any part of the mirror and concentrates it onto a **solar receiver** running along the middle. The receiver is the part that heats up. For a row of troughs, the receiver is usually a tube of oil. The oil heats to around 750°F (400°C) and is then pumped to a nearby power block. Here the hot oil flows through tubes in tanks of water. The water boils and the steam is used to generate power.

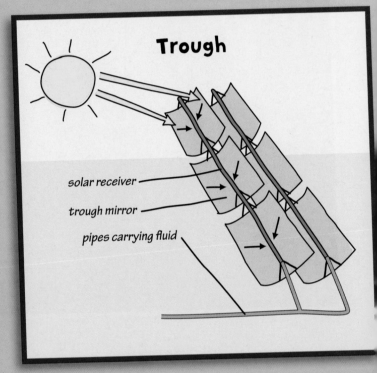

Trough

solar receiver

trough mirror

pipes carrying fluid

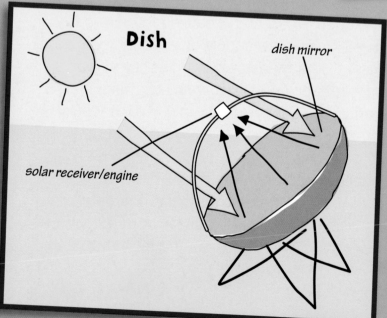

Dish

dish mirror

solar receiver/engine

Dishes

A solar dish works in a similar way but the receiver for each dish-shaped mirror is often a special device called a Stirling engine. When trapped air inside this engine is warmed and expands, it operates a generator.

Solar Towers

Other thermal solar plants have a single solar tower surrounded by a number of mirrors. Each mirror is flat and angled so that it reflects sunlight onto a receiver at the top of the tower. Tubes in the receiver contain melted salts that are different from the salt we eat. These salts can get twice as hot as oil and they also stay hot for a long time. The hot salts boil water in the same way as the hot oil, but they contain more heat energy.

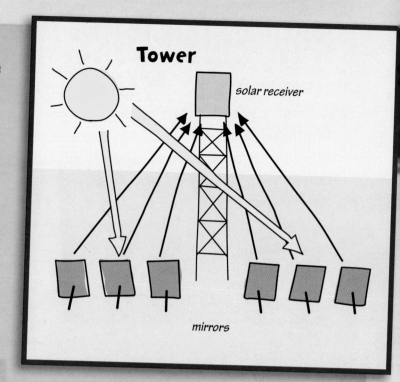

Tower

solar receiver

mirrors

"I am certain that the energy of the future is going to be thermal solar. There is nothing comparable. The sooner we focus on it the better."
Professor Jack Steinberger, Nobel prize-winning director of the CERN particle physics laboratory in Geneva, 2009

Using Rising Air

Some power companies have built thermal solar power systems that use rising hot air to make electricity rather than steam. A thermal updraft tower is something like a very large glass or plastic greenhouse with a tall chimney-shaped tower in the middle. Sunlight warms up the air beneath the glass so it expands and gets lighter. This warm air rises up the tower, spinning turbines in the tower that move generators, and generates electricity.

A solar tower receiver in a small thermal solar power station in Israel. Motors underneath the mirrors angle them up or down to direct sunlight.

How Solar Cells Work

A solar cell is a combination of special materials that are sandwiched together in layers. The layers work together to convert light energy from the Sun into electricity. This conversion of energy is called the **photovoltaic** effect. That is why solar cells are also known as photovoltaic or PV cells.

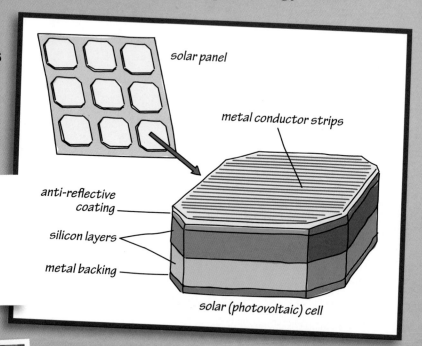

solar panel

metal conductor strips

anti-reflective coating

silicon layers

metal backing

solar (photovoltaic) cell

Solar cells together form solar panels. Glass or plastic on top of the cell protects the silicon inside. It also has a coating to stop useful light reflecting away from the cell.

Light Energy to Electricity

Most solar cells contain two very thin layers of silicon, a material that can be extracted from sand. The silicon in each layer is coated with a different chemical. When light energy hits the silicon layers, it makes a very small electric **current** start to flow between them. Metal strips on top of the cell **conduct** or carry the electricity away from the silicon layers to wires. The wires take the electricity to where it is needed. Individual solar cells are often connected together in **solar panels** to provide more power.

Silicon layers in solar cells are usually thin wafers cut by machine from large silicon crystals made in special factories.

Let's Discuss

Solar power is a better way to make electricity than fossil fuel power.

For:

No Fuel or Harmful Gases
To generate each megawatt of electricity, a coal power plant burns 3,086 tons (2,800 tonnes) of coal and releases nearly 6,614 tons (6,000 tonnes) of carbon dioxide.

Endless Massive Supply
The Sun will keep burning for millions of years. Enough solar energy hits Earth each second to provide all the world's energy needs for a year.

Against:

No Sunlight, No Power
Solar cells and thermal solar power stations do not work when the Sun is not shining.

Better than Coal
Many modern fossil fuel power plants burn gas, which releases two-thirds less carbon dioxide than coal.

Solar power is better than fossil fuel generation because it is renewable and does not cause global warming.

Solar panels are wired together to combine the electricity made by hundreds of connected solar cells.

How Solar Power Varies

Solar power can only be harnessed in the daytime and not at night. But the amount of solar power available also varies from day to day, from season to season, and between different places around the world.

Sun and Climate

The amount of solar power available to different countries around the world varies greatly depending on climate. Climate is the typical pattern of weather a place has throughout the year. For example, tropical climates are hot and sunny almost all year round. Climates such as those in Europe and most of North America have generally warm, sunny summers followed by cool, wet winters with fewer hours of sunlight.

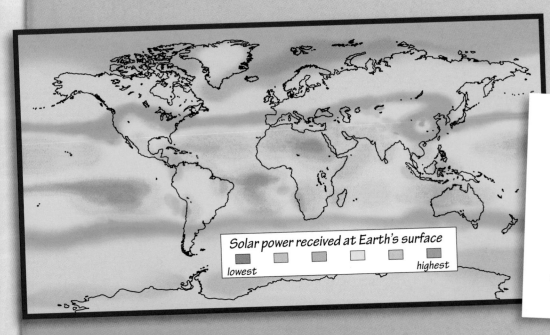

Solar power received at Earth's surface
lowest   highest

The greatest solar power is generally near the equator and away from the poles. However, this map shows that it varies between different areas of ocean and land.

Solar Power Availability

Places with sunny, hot climates can create electricity from solar power all year round. The problem for temperate places is that solar power generates more electricity in summer and less in winter. Scientists have not yet found a reliable way to store solar power generated on a sunny summer's day for use in winter. So solar power is not an ideal energy resource for people who need electricity to run heating and lighting systems on cold, dark winter evenings.

Storing Solar

Solar power can only be stored for fairly short periods of time. It is mainly stored to be used overnight or to top up other power sources on a cloudy day. One method of storing solar power is as electricity in **batteries**. The problem is that batteries are expensive and lose stored electricity quite quickly. A method used in thermal solar systems is to store solar power as heat. Melted salts are heated in towers and then kept in tanks that prevent them from losing heat.

These big towers store molten salt for the Solar Two power station in California.

CASE STUDY

Clouds, Global Warming, and Solar Power

Many scientists think that global warming is producing fewer clouds close to the Earth that normally reflect sunlight back into space. With fewer clouds, there would be more solar power, but also faster global warming. A study by the Copenhagen Consensus Center in 2009 concluded that we should make clouds to slow global warming. Special sailing ships could suck up seawater and spray it out of tall funnels high into the sky. Water vapor in the atmosphere would collect in clouds around the salty spray. A large fleet of these ships crossing the oceans could make enough cloud to reflect over 1 percent of sunlight that would otherwise warm the Earth.

Solar Cells for Different Needs

One of the important advantages of solar power is that it can be generated where it is needed. Solar cells can be installed on anything from a calculator to a space station, and from a tent to an office building. This kind of **microgeneration** allows families, small communities, and businesses to generate enough electricity for their own needs.

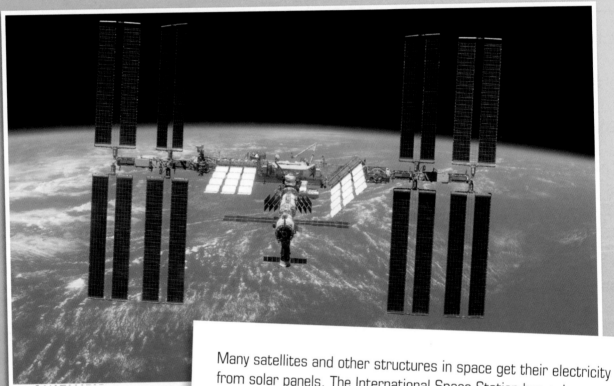

Many satellites and other structures in space get their electricity from solar panels. The International Space Station has solar panels the size of football fields to power all of its technology!

Remote Places

Around 1.5 billion people around the world do not have **household electricity**. This is mostly because they live in remote places that are not connected to a **grid**, which is the network of cables linking places to power stations in many countries. Solar panels are being introduced in many remote places in sunny countries across the world, from African villages to isolated farms in central Australia. It is much cheaper to supply panels than install cables and in some less developed countries, charities may help pay for the panels. Solar radios, computers, lights, pumps, and road signs are some of the many microgenerating devices that have a massive impact in remote places.

Built-in Power

In microgeneration, solar panels are erected close to or on the structures that will use the electricity they produce. Solar panels are often fixed to roofs of buildings or on the ground near a building. That way, there is no need for long cables to take the electricity to the people who use it. Solar panels are often angled so they face the Sun. Being angled also means rain and any dirt run off their surface. Modern buildings sometimes use special solar building materials instead of panels. These include roof tiles and window glass with built-in solar cells.

CASE STUDY   Barefoot College

Barefoot College, in the Indian state of Rajasthan, is helping poor, remote villages in India to use solar power. Villagers attend the college and are trained to be engineers. They learn how to set up and maintain solar cells. These engineers then take solar panels and electric lanterns, many made in the college using local materials, back to their villages. There are now over 400 engineers and they have introduced solar lighting to 12,000 homes and around 1,200 education centers. In the past, many children used to miss out on education because they spent their days tending to family cattle. Now they can continue with family duties and study useful skills such as math and reading at night schools that are lit up by solar lanterns.

Barefoot College employs local people with local knowledge to distribute, help set up, and educate villagers about solar power.

Solar Power Plants

Solar power stations, which are often called **solar farms**, consist of many solar panels or lots of mirrors linked together. A solar farm generates lots of electricity from one site. A grid takes the electricity from the solar power station to businesses, homes, and towns away from the site.

Where to Build a Solar Farm

A solar farm needs a large area of land for two reasons. First, there need to be enough mirrors or panels to harvest a large amount of solar radiation. Second, the mirrors and panels need to be spaced out so they do not shade each other. Power companies often build solar farms on wasteland, dry scrubland, or deserts. These types of land are usually cheap to buy and the land is fairly level.

The PS10 solar farm in Spain has 600 mirrors on 618 acres (250 hectares)—the size of 125 football fields—to generate electricity for 5,000 local homes.

Power companies usually bulldoze land to remove plants that might get in the way or shade mirrors or panels, and to make sure it is completely flat. Thermal solar plants need level ground so all of the mirrors can reflect lots of light, whatever the position of the Sun. An ideal site for thermal solar power stations also has a good water supply nearby, such as a river, to take water for making steam used to turn the turbines.

Are solar farms a good use of space?

No:

Less Power
A solar farm that generates 20MW of electricity takes up the same space as a coal power plant that makes five times more electricity.

Changing Places
Flattening land damages soil and natural **habitats**. Solar power plants use water that local plants and animals need.

Yes:

Lower Impact
Solar farms need no fuel to generate electricity. The land impacts of coal power plants include the huge areas miners dig up to find coal.

Using Unwanted Land
Solar farms are usually built on poor-quality land that is unsuitable for people to live on or farm.

Solar farms are an efficient way to use waste land, so long as power companies try to protect vulnerable habitats.

CASE STUDY

A New Farm in the Mojave Desert

A giant solar farm with 20,000 mirror dishes is being built in the Mojave Desert in California. It will generate up to 500 MW of electricity. However, many scientists say that clearing land here damages habitats where rare plants and animals, such as the desert tortoise, live. The power company says they are taking steps to treat the land carefully and the farm will only use a small amount of water from the area because they use Stirling engines (see page 8).

Solar Power and Pollution

When solar power plants are up and running and generating electricity, they do not produce any gases that are harmful to the atmosphere. However, making solar cells and building solar power stations does cause some pollution. This has impacts on both the atmosphere and on living things.

Releasing Greenhouse Gases

How does solar power create greenhouse gases? Solar cells are mostly made from silicon. To make silicon, factories burn coal to heat sand and turn it into silicon crystals. Burning coal releases carbon dioxide gas into the atmosphere. Making mirrors, solar towers, and the concrete needed to build thermal solar power stations also uses electricity. This mostly comes from fossil fuel power plants that release greenhouse gases. The trucks and other vehicles used to carry solar power parts and clear land for power stations burn diesel oil that also releases greenhouse gases.

This is a view inside a furnace showing red-hot silicon. Lots of energy from burning fuels is needed to melt silicon so it can be shaped into crystals.

Solar Cell Pollution

Different stages of solar cell production cause other kinds of pollution, too. Small amounts of poisonous substances are used in solar cells. Lead is used in the electrical parts of cells and panels, and cadmium is used instead of silicon in some cells. Both of these substances are only poisonous in large quantities. This becomes an issue if they build up in living things over time. A worker in a solar cell factory could breathe in tiny amounts of cadmium or lead when making cells over a long time and gradually become sick.

Let's Discuss

Solar power is less polluting than coal power.

Against:

Health Hazards
Substances used to make solar cells are health hazards, particularly for people who make the cells. Cadmium can cause **cancers** and weak bones.

Greenhouse Gases
Clearing land for solar farms can damage soil and plants that normally soak up some of the carbon dioxide from the atmosphere.

For:

Poisonous Fuels
Burning coal in power plants releases 300 times more cadmium into the air than making solar cells.

Less Gas
A silicon factory releases about 1.5 tons of carbon dioxide to make a ton of silicon cells. A coal plant would release 60 tons of carbon dioxide to generate the same amount as the cells.

On balance, solar power is far less polluting than coal power.

Mining rocks to extract metals such as lead used in solar cells produces holes and lots of waste rock. Rain can wash away remaining metals from the rock, poisoning rivers and lakes.

How Efficient Is Solar Power?

When we switch on an electric light, some electrical energy turns into light and some is wasted as it turns into heat. Like any other power technology, solar power wastes energy, too. Its **efficiency**—how much it wastes—depends on many things.

Comparing Efficiency

At the present time, most solar cells are made from silicon, which converts about one-fifth of the solar radiation reaching its surface into electricity. The other four-fifths is wasted. Some solar cells are made from different photovoltaic materials that waste only half of the energy they capture. Thermal solar power stations convert about a third of solar energy hitting their mirrors into electricity, which is as efficient as the conversion of coal into electricity in power plants. However, coal supplies are limited, whereas there is an endless supply of sunlight so wastage is not expensive. However, if solar power stations were more efficient, they could make more electricity.

Cables heat up because the metal they are made from slows the flow of current, so some electrical energy converts into heat.

Losing Energy

Not all the electricity made in a power plant reaches homes and businesses. About 7 percent of all electricity generated in power stations is lost as heat that escapes from cables as electricity travels through the grid. In general, longer cables lose more electricity than shorter cables. Solar farms are often built on land far from where people live, so they lose more electricity than power plants built nearer to cities.

Heat Effect

Solar cells do not use the heat in sunlight to make electricity. When the silicon layers get too hot, the heat can cause problems for solar cells because it stops the electric current from moving into the wires. This is a major reason why solar farms in deserts usually use mirrors. The hotter conditions help warm the solar receiver faster. Solar panel farms are better at generating electricity in bright, cool conditions, for example, in parts of Europe, North America, and Japan.

Looking After Solar Farms

Solar cells and mirrors generate less when they are shaded or dirty. Since solar panels are made of lots of small cells connected together, when light is blocked from just a few cells, they can prevent the whole panel from working. Power company workers look after solar farms by cutting down plants that may shade panels. They check that motors to make the mirrors move and to pump melted salt or oil through the pipes work properly. They may also clean the mirrors and cells.

A technician checks a mirror trough installation for any damage, dirt, or other problems that might affect its solar efficiency.

The Cost of Solar Power

The major cost of solar power for electricity is building the power stations or making and installing solar panels. Once this is done, the costs for running and looking after a solar power plant are low. What's more, there is no fuel to buy as there is for fossil fuel power generation.

Paying for Power

All power stations cost a lot to set up before they can start generating electricity. Power companies have to buy land and equipment such as turbines. Presently, it costs three times more to set up a solar plant than it costs to set up fossil fuel power plants.

Solar power stations cost more to set up partly because they use newer and more expensive technology. Silicon crystals used to make solar cells are very expensive. At present there are not many factories making silicon, but there are many companies wanting to buy silicon. It is used to make computer and cell phone parts, as well as solar panels. This means that silicon makers can charge a high price for their sought-after product. One reason why set-up costs for solar power should get cheaper in the future is that more solar panels will be made without silicon.

The costs of all the stages in silicon production, from the worker producing silicon crystals in a furnace to finished solar cells, all contribute to the final cost of solar power.

Is solar power too expensive?

There are good environmental reasons for using solar power, but is the cost of solar power too high for most **consumers**?

Yes:

Comparing Costs

Electricity from thermal solar power stations is five times more expensive than electricity from fossil fuel or nuclear power stations. Electricity from solar cells and panels is even more costly.

Expensive Renewable

Solar is more expensive than every other kind of renewable energy resource apart from wave power, which uses new technology to capture ocean energy.

No:

Unfair Comparisons

The cost of fossil fuel power does not include the effects of global warming. For example, governments give money to farmers whose crops have failed because of extreme weather.

Getting Cheaper

Solar power is getting cheaper all the time. Scientists are inventing more efficient and cheaper solar technology that will reduce costs.

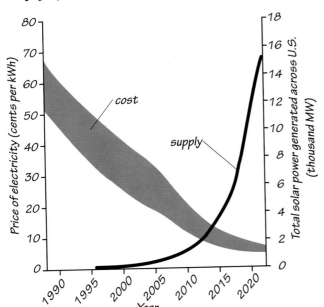

Supply and cost of solar power

The cost of solar power will get closer to other renewables and nonrenewables as the cost of solar technology falls.

The black line shows the possible increase in solar power into the future and the gray line shows how the price of electricity from solar power will probably fall.

Encouraging Solar Power Use

In an attempt to tackle global warming, representatives from governments around the world have met and agreed targets to reduce greenhouse gases released by their countries. To help them achieve these targets, many governments are encouraging solar power industries.

Helping to Set Up Solar Power

Governments can **subsidize** new solar projects to help set them up. They make payments or loans to help power companies and individuals pay for the costs of solar technology and installation. Governments may also ask fossil fuel power companies to reduce the greenhouse gases they create. Some power companies that previously relied only on fossil fuels have begun setting up solar farms or other renewable power plants that link in to their electricity grid to help them achieve this.

These climate protestors are asking the Canadian government to cut greenhouse gases. Slowing global warming will help protect the habitats where polar bears live.

Buying Excess Solar Electricity

Another way governments encourage solar power is to buy electricity that solar plants or panels generate. When solar power stations or solar panels make more electricity than they need, companies and individuals may feed the extra power into their regional electricity grid for others to use. It is easier to sell the spare electricity than store it for long periods of time in batteries. By paying for this renewable electricity, governments encourage companies and individuals to generate more.

**Solar Boom
in Germany**

In 2000, the German government decided to actively encourage solar power. It made a law to force power companies to pay more for electricity made using solar power than the price they normally sell fossil fuel electricity for. This caused a solar boom in Germany. Farmers put up solar panels in fields, individuals and businesses put panels on their roofs, and new solar companies were founded. By 2009, Germany had over half of the world's solar installations.

Let's Discuss **Solar power should be subsidized.**

Yes:

Encouraging Renewables
Encouraging renewables is not only cleaner but also fair, because many governments have subsidized nonrenewables such as fossil fuel power in the past.

Self-Sufficient
Using renewable power such as solar reduces a government's reliance on countries where fossil fuels are found.

No:

The Wrong Choice
If solar power is suitable to meet global power needs, then it shouldn't need subsidizing. It should survive on its own merits.

Hiding the True Cost
Subsidies come from money that people in a country pay their governments. Some people would prefer to choose which power technology to support.

It is a good idea for countries to subsidize solar in order to help develop an independent, clean, renewable power supply.

New Solar Technology

Solar power technology is quite new. The first solar cells that really worked appeared in the 1950s and thermal solar plants have only been around since the late 1980s. Here are some of the new solar technologies that are being developed today for future use.

Artificial Trees

Green leaves can use sunlight to make food for trees even when they are completely shaded. Scientists at Solar Botanic Energy Systems are trying to copy how all the leaves on a tree work together to turn sunlight into power. They plan to design 20 different types of artificial trees with different shapes and designs. The trees will have not only built-in solar cells but also technology to convert heat and the movement of leaves in the wind to make even more electricity!

The Solar Tree invented by Ross Lovegrove has solar panels built into the leaves that generate electricity by day to light the streets at night.

Reshaping Solar Power

The Cool Earth Solar company has invented a way to make solar power using balloons rather than flat solar panels. Their balloons are 8.2 feet (2.5 meters) wide, and rounded with clear tops. The curved top of a balloon, made from plastic, focuses sunlight onto the dark, reflective bottom. The light bounces off this toward a solar cell receiver at the top. The company says that their solar cell generates up to 400 times more electricity than other solar cells, for its size, because of the focusing effect of light in the balloon.

Solar Power in Space

Scientists are hoping to use vast satellites in space in the future to beam electricity from solar panels to Earth. In space, solar radiation is more powerful than at the Earth's surface since it has not had to travel through clouds and dust in the Earth's atmosphere. Also, building in space means there are fewer mirrors and panels covering the Earth's surface. It would not be possible to stretch power lines from space to Earth, so scientists plan to send the electrical energy as a beam of microwave radiation about 0.6 mi. (1 km) across. It remains to be seen whether power companies and governments are prepared to pay for this expensive technology and also whether it will actually work.

The Cool Earth Solar balloons can be constructed more cheaply and quickly than normal solar panels.

"We'll invest in the development and deployment of solar technology wherever it can thrive, and we'll find the best ways to integrate solar power into our electric grid."

President Barack Obama, 2009

CASE STUDY — Printing Solar Cells

The Nanosolar company, set up in 2002, makes solar cells without silicon by printing a special photovoltaic ink onto thin, flexible metal sheets. When sunlight shines on the ink, a current moves through the metal foil and the foil conducts the electricity to wires. Machines can print tens of yards of these "PowerSheets" each minute, and they cost about one-tenth the price of normal silicon cells for every watt they generate. Printed cells could be on all kinds of surfaces in the future, from car roofs to cell phones.

The Future for Solar Power

The cost of producing energy from renewables is falling and will continue to fall as more countries and individuals look to alternatives to fossil fuels. Meanwhile, the cost of fossil fuel power will rise. Because of this, solar power will undoubtedly be a growing part of the energy mix in future. Globally, some scientists believe that by 2050, solar power stations could produce up to one quarter of the world's electricity.

Increasing Availability

In the future, a combination of new technologies and more government commitment to renewable energy resources could bring a big increase in the use of solar power. As more countries invest in solar power and solar technology gets cheaper, more people will be able to afford solar electricity. Better methods for storing thermal solar heat and distributing solar-generated power will help these technologies meet demand. More efficient and adaptable solar panels may even be able to generate electricity to power more vehicles and cut the use of oil for fuel. Many people believe that it is simpler and cheaper to reduce how much electricity we use than switch to solar. We can all do this in many ways, from turning off lights when we leave a room to buying energy-efficient machines.

Bertrand Piccard invented the Solar Impulse airplane in 2009. Its 207-ft. (63-m) wingspan is covered with over 11,000 solar cells powering flight propellers.

Looking Ahead

Some regions of the world will expand their use of solar power faster than others. These are generally regions where there is plentiful sunlight, although governments may have different reasons for going solar. In some, such as North Africa, wind or running water are not so plentiful so solar power may be the only renewable energy resource available. In others, such as the United States, solar power will help reduce greenhouse gases and make the country less reliable on fuel from other countries.

Big businesses such as Walmart are installing solar panels on the roofs of some of their stores, such as this one in Palm Desert, California, as solar power grows in global popularity.

CASE STUDY

The Future Lies in the Desert

In the future, solar power could become more widely available if it can be transported from deserts where the sun is very strong and there are few clouds, to cooler temperate regions where the usage of electricity is high. There are plans to build a solar power network in the Sahara covering a total area the size of New Jersey. One of the biggest challenges is building new long-distance power transmission lines that do not lose much electricity. If the scheme works, experts believe that the countries of North Africa could supply enough electricity for almost all of Europe!

Solar Activity

Create a Solar Stove

You can make a very simple solar trough that collects enough sunlight to cook with. It works something like the thermal solar troughs on page 8.

It works something like the thermal solar troughs on page 8.

What you need:
- Shoebox without lid
- Thin card such as half an office folder
- Tape
- Aluminum foil
- Ruler
- Bamboo barbecue skewer longer than the box
- Marshmallows

1 Drape the card over the box so it hangs down in a half pipe shape and tape in place.

2 Smooth the foil over the card and tape down the edges.

3 Measure half the depth from the top of the box to the bottom of the trough, and draw a line at this level on the outside end of the box. **CAREFULLY** push the skewer through the box on this line, exactly half way across the box end. Thread marshmallows on before pushing the skewer out the other end.

4 Put the box outside on a sunny day and angle it toward the Sun. The shape of the trough will reflect sunlight onto the marshmallows and melt them!

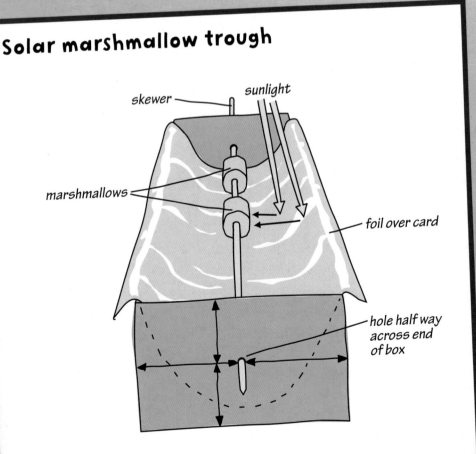

Solar marshmallow trough

skewer —
sunlight
marshmallows —
foil over card
hole half way across end of box

Solar Topics and Glossary

History
• People were using technology, such as magnifying glasses and mirrors, to heat things using the Sun's radiation in ancient Greek and Roman times. Make a timeline of how people have used solar power since then.

Geography
• Many different factors affect how hot or sunny a place is apart from its position on the Earth. Research altitude, albedo effect, and smog.

Design and Technology
• What features would a solar-powered car or airplane need? Design your own solar-powered vehicle. For some inspiration, find out about the Solar Challenge car race and the recent Solar Impulse airplane (see picture on page 28).

English
• Write an imaginary diary from the year 2200 describing life without coal, gas, and oil, but with widespread renewable power.

Science
• Find out about the effects of global warming on the following ecosystems: Arctic sea ice, coral reefs.

Glossary

atmosphere mix of gases surrounding the Earth up to the edge of space.

battery store of electrical energy.

cancer disease in which abnormal cells grow and kill normal body cells.

carbon dioxide gas found in air that is produced by living things, or by burning fossil fuels.

conduct allow electricity to pass through. Copper in electric wires conducts well.

consumer person who buys services or products such as electricity or cars.

current flow of electricity.

efficiency when resources, such as energy, are used wisely and are not wasted.

fossil fuel fuel such as coal formed over millions of years from remains of living things.

global warming increase in the average temperature of the Earth's atmosphere and oceans.

greenhouse gas gas such as carbon dioxide that stores heat in the atmosphere.

grid system of power lines and pylons for sending electricity across a wide area.

habitat place where particular types of animals or plants normally live.

household electricity electricity supplied through the grid to users from power plants.

kinetic energy energy produced by movement.

microgeneration small-scale production of electricity to meet the needs of users.

nonrenewable energy resource such as coal that is running out as it is not replaced when used.

photovoltaic with the property of converting sunlight into electricity.

pollution harmful substances that make air, water, or soil less safe to use or live in.

power plant (station) factory for generating electricity.

radiation energy that moves in narrow lines or rays.

renewable energy resource that is replaced naturally and can be used without running out.

solar cell device usually containing silicon that converts solar to electrical energy.

solar farm area with many solar thermal mirrors or solar panels to generate electricity.

solar panel structure containing solar cells linked together to increase electricity output.

solar receiver part of solar thermal system that mirrors focus heat upon.

subsidize pay to support something and encourage its success.

turbine machine for converting linear into mechanical kinetic energy.

Further Information, Web Sites, and Index

Books

Energy for the Future and Global Warming: Solar Power
by Anne Rooney
(Gareth Stevens Publishing, 2007)

Energy Now and in the Future: Solar Power
by Neil Morris
(Smart Apple Media, 2009)

The World of Energy: Understanding Solar Power
by Fiona Reynoldson
(Gareth Stevens Publishing, 2010)

Web Sites

Due to the changing nature of Internet links, PowerKids Press has developed an online list of Web sites related to the subject of this book. This site is updated regularly. Please use this link to access this list:
http://www.powerkidslinks.com/lder/solar/

Index